MILLION-DOLLAR SALES CONVERSATIONS GUIDEBOOK

Million-Dollar Sales Conversations

By Mike Klein

978-0-9905975-1-3 - ISBN Guidebook
978-0-9905975-0-6 - ISBN Paperback

Sales *Edge* Publishing

MILLION DOLLAR SALES CONVERSATIONS

THE GUIDEBOOK

MIKE KLEIN

TABLE OF CONTENTS

MILLION-DOLLAR SALES CONVERSATIONS

This guidebook is based on the Million-Dollar Sales Conversations book. The book along with this guidebook provides a process for building great opportunities through million-dollar sales conversations.

This guidebook is for anyone who sells, and that includes you, even if you're not in what's technically considered to be a sales job. We all sell something. We sell ourselves during job interviews, business meetings, dinner dates, school, block parties, and so forth. Teachers have to "sell" students by motivating them to study. Politicians need to sell their proposed bills. You have to sell yourself every time you interact with people. If you're not interesting or expressing interest in others, no one wants to be around you.

No matter what industry you work in, you've probably seen some people rise to the top very quickly. They have some sort of charisma that draws people to them. So what do they have that you don't? Absolutely nothing. It's simply that they have mastered the art of the million-dollar sales conversation. The idea of a million-dollar sales conversation means different things to different people. The goal may not be a million-dollar sale, but it might be something that represents what you view as the ultimate prize. It could be a first order, a new contact, a referral, or a meeting with a top executive. It could be a chance to lead a project. It could be a chance to interview for a new job or to accept one.

The Process

In the *Million-Dollar Sales Conversations Guidebook,* you will be presented with the process for building great opportunities through your conversations. Each of the steps correlates with a chapter from the book. You may use the book as a guide as you work your way through the planner. The process steps are listed below:

Chapter 1 – The Million-Dollar Sales Conversation: Open Up Relationships before Trying to Make a Sale!

Chapter 2 – The Attitude of a Conversation

Chapter 3 – Look Toward the Horizon: Figuring Out Your Goals

Chapter 4 – Active Listening

Chapter 5 – Encouragement for Yourself, Your Sales Staff, and Your Customers

Chapter 6 – Conversation Starters: Making Small Talk

Chapter 7 – Awaken and Expand Your Network

Chapter 8 – Action Steps to Take Conversations to the Next Level

The Million-Dollar Sales Conversation: Open Up Relationships before Trying to Make a Sale!

Introduction

Until we realize just how outdated traditional views of selling are, finding yourself in the middle of that million-dollar conversation is going to be difficult. So how do we get into such a conversation? How do we land that major deal? How do we get people engaged with us and move them to want to be engaged at the highest level? Having million-dollar conversations and getting people to invest large amounts of time and money on what we are selling is a process, and it can be learned and mastered!

Selling Yourself

Exercise #1

First, you've got to figure out exactly what you're selling—and that something is you! Don't get confused. You need to spend time knowing the products you represent and the value they bring to the customer. However, salespeople sometimes forget that selling is about connecting with people and building trust. It is critical that you understand how to solve your customer's needs and sell yourself. The great thing about selling yourself is that you are already an expert on you. Once you're aware of this, you can then begin seeking out how to build meaningful business relationships that can lead to those million-dollar sales conversations.

Before you can "sell" yourself, you need to have a clear understanding about yourself. In this exercise, you will provide a sales pitch about....YOU! In your sales pitch, you will describe your key characteristics, discuss who you are (strengths and opportunities), and explain your sales approach.

Conversations and Relationships

Making a sale all started with creating a conversation that would engage your prospect in a meaningful way. Sometimes these conversations led to meaningful relationships, and other times they didn't. When one human being makes an honest attempt to engage with another for purposes that transcend selling, the relationship will have a stronger bond.

Ultimately, the more opportunities you create for conversations, the more chances you have to build meaningful relationships. Creating meaningful relationships is one of the essential keys to developing a million-dollar sales conversation. Each successful sales opportunity starts with a conversation—learn about your prospects and what *matters* to them.

The best way to do this is to put yourself in your prospect's shoes. Concentrate on how you come across in conversations, and be aware of your word choices. Your conversations should focus on figuring out a prospect's needs and wants, not on overcoming his or her objections. Make sure you're asking questions that matter, and that show you're on the same page as your prospect. Test him or her for reactions, and paraphrase what he or she has said to you and repeat it back to the person to show you truly do understand his or her concerns. This is what it takes to be in a million-dollar conversation.

Exercise #2

For this exercise, you will identify the needs/wants of the prospect. In addition, you will provide a response to the prospect based on the situation that has been explained.

Prospect: My organization is looking to purchase new computers for their whole company for our employees. They don't have any idea what they need and understand they have several options (tablets, notebooks, smartphones and desktops). The company has a very tight budget. They need to prove the computers will drive productivity and performance in order to get approval to move forward with the purchase. We are just not sure which direction to go and we may not even purchase anything if we cannot stay within our budget.

Sales Don't Begin or End with Sale

Through all of these years of selling, the lesson has been the same. Start with a conversation that leads to a relationship. Look for some commonalities (e.g., you both went to the same school, you both have an interest in football, you both like theatre), and go from there. The key is inserting the personal side and the social side of you at the beginning of the buying process, not the end of it. High-performing salespeople use their social skills to get to know their customers over a long period of time. They build a relationship by gaining the customer's trust and getting in at the beginning of the decision-making process. High-performing salespeople are more than just order takers; they're trusted advisors—customers share valuable intellectual capital with them so the best possible solutions can be found.

Each time you have a conversation with a potential customer, you get a chance to know the person better. You also have a chance to set yourself apart and put yourself in a position to truly help him or her. Taking an interest in your customer's goals, objectives, needs, wants, and desires helps you create an environment to build the right solutions.

You can't get to know potential customers overnight. This is the sort of thing that comes with time and practice. You may consider starting with the people you already know. Believe it or not, there are probably many things you don't already know about them. In fact, you may discover a common interest upon which you both can build.

Successful salespeople aren't just focused on closing the deal. They have time and effort invested in the outcome because they have opened up conversations that lead to relationships, forming bonds with their customers. And the term "salesperson" doesn't apply only to people who consider themselves to be in the business of selling. As I have pointed out, everyone has something to sell. It's all about *initiative.*

Exercise #3

For this exercise, you will have the opportunity to develop 10 questions that you would ask prospects when you first meet them. Remember, the key to the sale is getting to know your potential customers and starting to build the rapport and the relationship. Write your questions below:

1. _____

2. _____

3. _____

4. _____

5. _____

6. _____

7. _____

8. _____

9. _____

10. _____

Introduction

Have you ever had a conversation with someone who had a great attitude? How did that conversation go? How did you feel about that conversation? How engaged were you in that conversation? What did you think about that person? Did you want to spend more or less time with that person?

So what is the bottom line here? You need to teach yourself to be positive at all times. In other words, it's all about your attitude. As Winston Churchill once said, "Attitude is a little thing that makes a big difference."

All About Attitude

I'm sure you have heard this before—people buy from people they like. People like having conversations, relating to others and building connections. People with whom you do business are just people, like you. Your attitude about your interactions with people is a lot more than just about the current agenda at hand. You will build strong and lasting relationships by having conversations that *engage* other people. You have to develop a positive attitude in your interactions with others because they can feel and see when you are sincere.

How can you make sure you show up effectively? Prepare. Take time each day to prepare your attitude to be *responsive* rather than *reactive*. Whether it's telling yourself in a mirror every morning, "You're great! You're great! You're great!" or listening to motivational podcasts or reading inspirational passages from any number of books, I guarantee you that these practices will make you smile, and they will also change your attitude.

Exercise #1

Think about your attitude. How do you come across to others? Don't take a guess. Instead, ask people at least three people you know over the next couple of days the following question: "How do I normally come across to you and others?" Record their responses below. In addition, describe your reaction to their comments. Are you surprised? Is this what you expected?

Response #1

_____

_____

_____

Response #2

_____

_____

_____

Response #3

_____

_____

_____

Your Reaction

_____

_____

_____

_____

_____

_____

Partner-Building Attitude

When you're looking out for the needs of your customers, it's important to realize that they are *people* first, even when they represent a large company. The best relationship you can have with them is that of a partner. When a prospect asks you to do something, he or she is testing you. The way you respond to his or her request will help determine your ability to cultivate a positive or negative relationship. Whenever it is possible, you should say something like, "It would be my pleasure to do that."

Exercise #2

Mary Kay Ash, founder of Mary Kay Cosmetics, provided the following advice to her salespeople: "Pretend that every single person you meet has a sign around his or her neck that says, 'Make me feel important.' Not only will you succeed in sales, you will succeed in life." This is a surefire way to build relationships with contacts and customers. In this exercise, you will brainstorm how you can make your customers feel important. Record your ideas below:

1. _____
2. _____
3. _____
4. _____
5. _____
6. _____
7. _____
8. _____
9. _____
10. _____

Personalized Relationships

Mother Teresa said many wonderful and inspiring things while she was alive, but this statement from her captures the essence of what you should strive for in every relationship: "Let no one ever come to you without leaving better and happier." The key to making customers feel better and happier is to cultivate friendships with them so your extensive business knowledge can benefit them on a regular basis. Here are the steps to building solid, long-lasting business relationships from the start:

1. **Create a relationship.** Do this by starting with great conversations.
2. **Personalize the relationship**. Connect by looking for personal things that matter to the person with whom you are connecting.
3. **Cultivate the relationship.** Do little things for your contacts that you know they will like. Spend time with them in a nonbusiness environment.
4. **Sustain the relationship.** Take time at least once a month to touch base with them. Consider sending your connections articles of interest, or just check in to see how they are doing. Also, remember to wish them happy birthday and to congratulate them when it is appropriate.
5. **Expand the relationship.** Stay connected as if they are your friend. Call with no other agenda but to see how they are doing. Invite them to a sporting event or concert.

Exercise #3

As we discussed in Chapter Two, there are five main types of relationships you will create. For each type of relationship, discuss ideas for personalizing and building the relationship.

Acquaintances

_____

_____

Contacts

_____

_____

Personal Relationships

_____

_____

Prospects

_____

_____

Partnerships

_____

_____

_____

CHAPTER 3

Look Toward the Horizon: Figuring Out Your Goals

Introduction

Goal setting is the key to success in life, not just selling. But the big problem for many people is that they set goals they either can't or never intend to meet. For example, did you know that 25 percent of those who set New Year's resolutions abandon them just a week after they set those goals? In fact, 60 percent of them dump their resolutions entirely within 6 months. Also, the average person makes the same New Year's resolution 10 different times without finding success. So what do these statistics tell us about setting goals? They tell us that not only is it very difficult to meet our goals, but few people achieve them even when they do set them. Those who do achieve their goals may be in the minority, but it's possible.

Successfully Setting Goals

Successful goal setters *write their goals down*. It's not enough to *set* goals. You've got to see them in black and white in front of your eyes. If you don't take the time to write them down, then it becomes too easy to forget about them, ignore them, or just plain abandon them entirely.

To circumvent failure and all of these struggles it helps to know why you're setting your goals.

1. **Setting goals forces you to clarify what you want.** Without knowing your destination, you can't make progress toward getting what you want.
2. **Setting goals motivates you to take action.** Writing your goals down is only the beginning. Writing your goals down does require you to articulate your intention.

3. **Setting goals also provides a filter for other opportunities.** When you clearly see your goal in front of you it's easy to steer clear of opportunities which are actually distractions rather than stepping stones.

4. **Setting goals helps you overcome resistance.** Every meaningful intention, dream, or goal encounters resistance. The way to overcome it is to focus on the goal—the thing you want.

5. **Setting goals enables you to see—and celebrate—your progress.** Life is hard. It is particularly difficult when you aren't seeing much, if any, progress. There is strength and hope in seeing how much the distance from our beginning to our goal has been reduced!

Exercise #1

Goal setting is very important to your success now and in the future. For this exercise, create a list of your personal and professional goals. Please write your goals below:

Personal

1. _____
2. _____
3. _____
4. _____
5. _____

Personal

1. _____
2. _____
3. _____
4. _____
5. _____

Make Addressing Your Goals a Daily Habit

Your goals should be very specific and measurable. Often the acronym SMART is used: specific, measurable, achievable, relevant, and time-bound.

The reason for these guidelines is simple. Goals that are too vague are difficult to keep, and they certainly aren't measurable. How do you know when you've made progress toward your goal if you can't measure it? Unmeasurable goals can be a source of frustration because you can't see how far you have come. You don't really know if you're moving toward your goal, or spinning your wheels and staying in place. If you set the bar too high, it's easy to get frustrated as well. Having a timeline in which you want to achieve your goals is helpful because it's part of the measurement process. In addition to the SMART acronym, it's also a good idea to set short-term milestones on the way to your long-term goals. Break down those longer goals into smaller steps or milestones, and set a time frame in which you want to achieve each milestone. Then, get moving!

Exercise #2

For this exercise, you will use the personal and professional goals that you created in exercise #1. For each of your 10 goals, break them down using the SMART acronym. In addition, create short-term milestones for each of the 10 goals.

	PERSONAL GOAL #1	PERSONAL GOAL #2	PERSONAL GOAL #3	PERSONAL GOAL #4	PERSONAL GOAL #5
Specific					
Measurable					
Attainable					
Realistic					
Time Bound					
Short-Term Milestones					

	PROFESSIONAL GOAL #1	PROFESSIONAL GOAL #2	PROFESSIONAL GOAL #3	PROFESSIONAL GOAL #4	PROFESSIONAL GOAL #5
Specific					
Measurable					
Attainable					
Realistic					
Time Bound					
Short-Term Milestones					

Remember the step-by-step process every time you go through the goal-setting process.

1. Write down your goals.
2. Read your goals every day.
3. Share your goals with a friend and give them regular progress reports.
4. Examine every opportunity that comes your way.
5. Realize that you will face resistance.
6. See resistance as yet another opportunity.
7. Celebrate your progress along the way.
8. Remind yourself of your goals every single day.
9. Create a roadmap of sub-goals or stepping stones.
10. Evaluate and review your goals on a regular basis.

CHAPTER 4

Active Listening

Introduction

So what's the difference between hearing and listening? Of course hearing is the (somewhat) physical action that occurs when your eardrums vibrate and sound waves travel through the air, into your ears, and to your brain. Listening is what happens when you actually hear *and comprehend* what the other person is saying.

It's pretty easy to say that listening is important. After all, how are you going to fulfill a customer's needs if you don't listen to what they say? Researchers also say we talk at a rate of 125 to 175 words per minute and listen at a rate of 125 to 250 words per minute but think at a rate of 1,000 to 3,000 words per minute. Researchers say the gap between these rates unfortunately creates opportunities for us to become distracted and, thus, fail to listen carefully to what the speaker is saying. So how can we reduce the distractions and stay focused on what our customers are saying? If you're coming up empty on ideas, you're not alone. The ILA also found that less than 2% of professionals have actually had formal education or training to understand and improve their listening skills and techniques. So, let's do something about this.

Active Listening & Sales

Actively listening is the key to being able to build dialogue in the meeting. Listening engages each person in the meeting on an ongoing basis during the meeting. If you aren't actively listening to what the members of the meeting are saying, you will never be able to build solutions that support their goals. Having million dollar sales conversations will not happen if you don't engage your listeners.

So to sum it up, there are six main reasons active listening is so important when it comes to maneuvering yourself into Million Dollar Conversations:

1. It makes you a better communicator.
2. It keeps others engaged with you.
3. It helps you avoid misunderstanding what the customer wants or needs.
4. It gets customers to open up and share more about what they want or need.
5. It keeps customers from getting defensive or becoming more defensive if they already were.
6. It enables you to build a relationship, which of course should be your goal every time you speak with a customer—whether or not you believe the customer is about to buy from you or not.

Exercise #1

One of the biggest obstacles we face when it comes to active listening is the distractions that are all around us. For this exercise, list your top 5 distractions that you face. In addition, brainstorm ideas for ways to eliminate these distractions in order to become a better listener.

Distraction #1 _____

Ways to eliminate distraction: _____

_____

_____

Distraction #2 _____

Ways to eliminate distraction: _____

_____

_____

Distraction #3 _____

Ways to eliminate distraction: _____

_____

_____

Distraction #4 _____

Ways to eliminate distraction: _____

_____

_____

Distraction #5 _____

Ways to eliminate distraction: _____

_____

_____

Active Listening & Body Language

Author Peter Drucker hit on one of the key elements of active listening when he said, "The most important thing in communication is hearing what isn't said." Taking in a customer's body language will reveal volumes about what they're really saying. It takes you beyond their words and gives you a picture of what they really mean. By noticing the kinds of physical signals the customer is giving off and also his tone of voice, you'll be able to gather some clues about how you might be able to help.

Does the customer look agitated? Is he standing with his arms folded or his stance more open? Does she look confused? Is she fidgeting? Does she look nervous? What about the customer's tone of voice? Is there an edge to it? Is there a smile accompanying the words? It will take some practice, but with a little bit of work, these sorts of questions will become second nature to you, not requiring any thinking on your part. You'll begin to notice these things automatically.

By listening carefully you're able to identify that what they're describing is different than the thing they actually said they wanted. Only through active listening, interpretation, and asking further questions about the customer's wants will you be able to get to the heart of the problem and provide the best possible solution.

Exercise #2

Understanding your customer's body language is important because you can learn a lot from body language. In this exercise, you will be given different types of body language. By each of the different types, describe what the body language type would tell you.

GESTURE:	MEANING:
Brisk, erect walk	
Standing with hands on hips	
Sitting with legs crossed, foot kicking slightly	
Sitting, legs apart	
Arms crossed on chest	
Walking with hands in pockets, shoulders hunched	
Hand to cheek	

GESTURE:	MEANING:
Touching, slightly rubbing nose	
Rubbing the eye	
Hands clasped behind back	
Locked ankles	
Head resting in hand, eyes downcast	
Rubbing hands	
Sitting with hands clasped behind head, legs crossed	
Open palm	

To check your responses, visit the following website for details on each gesture. http://listverse.com/2007/11/08/25-examples-of-body-language/

Not only should you be picking up on body language and tone of voice, but you should also look for unconscious gestures or behaviors. These unconscious gestures may provide better insight into what the other person is really thinking if you learn how to interpret them. The person you're speaking with may not even be totally aware of how they feel about the subject they're talking about. But the subconscious always knows. If you listen beyond their words, you may actually be able to help them figure out how they feel. This is something psychologists, therapists, and psychiatrists learn to master in order to help patients deal with problems.

Practicing Active Listening

So how can we move beyond these barriers, understand gestures, and personal habits to hone our active listening skills? This is indeed something that will take practice. I would advise you not to try to tackle every one of the problems we have discussed all at the same time. Ask someone who knows you well to help you figure out which of the issues is the most problematic for you. Then choose just one or two to work on at a time. It helps to check in regularly with the person you have chosen to help you. Ask them to hold you accountable for making progress and to help you keep track of where you are on your journey to become a better listener.

Exercise #3

For the next conversation you have with a prospect or current customer, practice the suggestions you have learned about active listening. And put the following suggestions into action:

1. **Avoid filtering what the other person said through your own biases**. If you find your internal voice starting to weigh too heavily on the other person's words, refocus your attention and look at it from their point of view.
2. **Actively take part in conversations.** Don't just rephrase what the other person has said but also taking in tone and body language and asking questions to show interest and better understand the other person's point of view and problem. Empathize if it's appropriate.
3. **Listen more than you talk.** Allow the other person's words to fully breathe so that you can respond rather than react to everything they have just said.
4. **Stop what you're doing and listen slowly.** You'll hear everything clearly and can take in cues other than the words that are actually being said. This also shows respect for the customer. Never, ever answer your cell phone in the middle of a conversation.
5. **Identify your bad listening habits and external listening barriers and then work on eliminating them.** Role-play and do exercises to banish bad habits and look for practical solutions to external listening barriers.

Now, after this conversation, record your thoughts on the conversation. Was the conversation better and more productive? Which of the following six steps did you work on during the conversation?

_____

_____

_____

_____

_____

_____

_____

_____

_____

_____

_____

_____

_____

_____

_____

_____

_____

_____

_____

_____

_____

_____

CHAPTER 5

Encouragement for Yourself, Your Sales Staff, and Your Customers

Introduction

Encouragement can be as simple as a pat on the back and an admonition to "hang in there," or taking time to counsel and console and mentor someone through a tough time.

When it comes to building relationships, encouragement is an important part of the equation. Encouragement is also essential in all aspects of the sales process, whether it involves encouraging yourself after you took a hit, encouraging your customer or contacts, or encouraging your sales staff or coworkers. So what exactly does encouragement look like? Of course it depends on the situation, but there is a general guideline to keep in mind when you're looking for ways to encourage anyone.

Steven R. Covey, author of *The 7 Habits of Highly Effective People*, said, "Treat a man as he is and he will remain as he is. Treat a man as he can and should be and he will become as he can and should be."

So essentially, encouragement should involve treating the person the way he or she can and should be. If it's a potential customer or contact, there can be a broad range of areas in which you can encourage the person.

Self-Encouragement

As I share in my book I mention that encouragement can be as simple as a pat on the back or a sincere "thank you" for doing a good job that day. It could also be a reminder to the person how great he or she is and how much you appreciate them being part of your team.

There will be times when you need encouragement and there's no one around to encourage you. You'll need to learn to encourage yourself. Encouraging yourself can take several different forms. This is something personal that only you can decide what works.

Sales slumps happen to the best salespeople. To break a sales slump, listen to motivational tapes or post inspirational quotes where you will see them on a regular basis. This type of encouragement should take place on a daily basis, even if you're not in a slump. It can actually help lessen the severity of a slump or cut down on how often you experience a sales slump. If you get into a slump, change your routine. Do something different. Take another approach. If you're already down it can't get worse so take a few risks. Something is bound to reset and get you rolling again. Remind yourself slumps happen. It's as much a part of the sales process as summer and winter are parts of the seasons.

Exercise #1

Self-encouragement is important because many times you will not have people around you to encourage you. For this exercise, discuss ways that you encourage yourself. Be specific about the activities you already use and activities that you would like to try.

Current Encouragement Techniques

1. _____

2. _____

3. _____

4. _____

5. _____

Techniques You Would Like to Try

1. _____

2. _____

3. _____

4. _____

5. _____

Encouraging Customers

Encouragement is an important part of every relationship, whether personal or professional. It not only shows the other person that you care about them and care about how well they perform on their goals, but it also demonstrates that you know them well enough to speak about their problems. Offering encouragement enables you to support your contacts when they have issues by helping them find the best solution possible.

Sometimes you may not even be dealing with a problem at all. In these cases, you might simply have an opportunity to advance a relationship by just making people feel good about themselves. Your encouragement may give them the courage to explore new things or discover hidden talents. After all, sometimes people just need encouragement, whether it's because they're going through a difficult time or they're unsure of where they're going next.

Exercise #2

For exercise #2, we will use the case study presented in Chapter Five. Please re-read the case study below:

Case Study—One of the Best Salespeople of All Time: Erica vanderLinde Feidner

Inc.com and CBS Moneywatch both put together lists of the best salespeople of all time. Erica vanderLinde Feidner landed on both lists, essentially because she was such an excellent encourager of salespeople. Before she became the owner of PianoMatchmaker. com, she was Steinway & Sons' top salesperson around the globe for eight years in a row. She moved more than $41 million worth of pianos priced between $2,000 and $152,000.

Feidner was exceptional at diagnosing what type of customer she was working with and adapting her sales approach to match each customer. Some customers who considered buying pianos were new to music. They were hesitant to buy an instrument because of all the time it would take to learn to play the piano. Experienced piano players see pianos as very personal items they will use for hours on end every single day and don't hesitate to invest. Of course, it's obvious that these two types of customers are worlds apart. There is a whole host of customers who fall somewhere in between those two extremes.

According to the report from CBS Moneywatch, Feidner utilized her teaching skills to work with customers who were considering learning how to play. She worked with them for an hour, giving them a basic lesson so that they could be playing a song on the piano by the time the impromptu lesson was over. For experienced players, she considered every piano's personality and focused on matching the perfect piano with the perfect person. In considering a piano's personality, she thought about the age of the instrument, how to take care of it, the materials it is made from and, most importantly, how it sounded.

In a 1999 article in *The New Yorker*, one of Feidner's customers, journalist James B. Stewart, said many customers saw her as "a force of nature." He said she didn't pressure clients, but rather that after meeting her, many soon find themselves in the grip of musical ambitions they never knew they harbored." In other words, she encouraged customers to develop their piano-playing skills.

Based on this case study, what were Feidner's techniques for encouraging her customers? List the techniques you noted from the case study below:

_____

_____

_____

_____

_____

_____

_____

_____

_____

_____

_____

_____

_____

_____

_____

Consider your own customers, brainstorm techniques for encouraging your employees. How can you encourage your customers and help them to say "yes" to your products?

1. _____

2. _____

3. _____

4. _____

5. _____

CHAPTER 6

Conversation Starters: Making Small Talk

Introduction

People buy people, not products or services. That's why word of mouth advertising is so incredibly valuable. People buy from people they know, like and trust. They don't develop that trust until they get to know you, and they don't get to know you until they've had a chance to talk to you and build a relationship. Building a relationship with a prospect or customer is a lot like making friends and building relationships anywhere. It starts with 'small talk.' You've got to:

1. **Make a good first impression.** Relax, smile, look people in the eye, be genuine.
2. **Let go of any judgments about the person you're meeting.** Don't focus on their clothes, their age, race, sexual orientation, body type or appearance. Don't dismiss or prejudge someone because of their looks. You really can't judge a book, or a person, by their cover.
3. **Pay attention.** Pay attention to the person, to anyone with them, to their environment, their clothing (not in a judgmental way), and everything that is happening around them. Are they in a suit? Or surf shorts? Are they wearing a T-shirt with a photo or slogan on it that you can ask them about? Do they have military or other tattoos that might have a story behind them? If you have the chance to Google someone, or their company before speaking with them, do so. Learn as much as you can about them before you meet them when possible. Use that information as an icebreaker. If they've just come into your store or showroom, notice their demeanor. Do they seem rushed or relaxed? Are they 'just looking' or do they head directly to a certain section of the store? Simply saying, "You seem like you're in a hurry. May I help you?" lets them know you value their time and thus sparks trust.

4. **Be genuinely interested and curious about people.** Ask questions. Don't interrogate, but do pursue your curiosity. A great place to do this is in lines at stores. People generally welcome small talk to make the time pass. Ask about an item in their shopping cart. Ask them if they like it, or what they like about it. You can practice these skills anywhere.

Exercise #1

You know now that good relationships are where the best sales opportunities lie. But breaking the ice with a potential customer can be one of the hardest things to do, for one or more reasons:

❏ **You're shy, introverted or not really a people person.** Shy and introverted people actually make some of the best salespeople because they naturally shut up and let the customer talk and generally think about what they want to say before they say it. If you're not a people person you can learn to be with practice.

❏ **You haven't thought about sales as a conversation before.** Old habits die hard. If you've been in sales for a long time you may find it difficult, confusing, or even scary to change the way you approach prospects.

❏ **You are afraid to be vulnerable.** Most of us have been taught all our lives to protect ourselves, to not open up, to not be vulnerable. That's understandable in the corporate world or where being vulnerable can be risky. But the fact is, it's that vulnerability and willingness to open up to customers that helps us establish trust. When people see we're willing to be vulnerable with them they think, "He must trust me. It's safe to trust him back." It's our vulnerability, openness and willingness to share ourselves with others that creates the emotional connections we need for a successful sales relationship.

❏ **You don't like or 'do' chit-chat.** Not everyone likes chit-chat. Many salespeople like to get right down to business, but not every customer does. The problem with not liking to talk to people can come across as judgmental, alienating or like you feel annoyed or bothered by the customer's questions or conversation.

❏ **You don't understand various social styles.** You may be aware that introverted and extroverted people are different. Introverts tend to be quiet, avoid being the center of attention and listen more than talk. Extroverts tend to thrive on being with people, talking and being the center of attention. But there are other social styles to consider as well.

Your personality probably fits into one of the personality types described above. For this exercise, discuss your personality. In addition, discuss the barriers that you feel your personality presents for starting conversations. List your responses below:

_____

_____

_____

_____

_____

_____

_____

_____

_____

_____

_____

_____

_____

_____

_____

_____

_____

_____

Noble Sales Purpose

If your sales goal is all about numbers, you're not only missing the point, you're most likely missing the sale. Helping your customer solve their problem, whether it's weight loss, monitoring their health, getting organized, remodeling a room in their home, or streamlining their business, you have to have both a noble purpose and sales staff and employees who embrace it. Many people may see "noble selling" as an oxymoron, but it's not. Customers are people, not targets to be acquired, or wallets to plunder.

Figure out what problems your product or service solves or can solve. Noble Sales purposes are the things that drive a company's employees to love their job.

Examples of noble purposes:

- Help families monitor their loved one's diabetes, heart and blood pressure problems from a distance
- Help customers lose weight
- Help customers streamline their businesses
- Help customers get organized
- Help customers... what else?

See a keyword here? It's help! Find a way to convert what you do into a "helping" phrase and chances are you've found your noble purpose.

Exercise #2

For this exercise, consider the products/services that your company offers or that you are specifically responsible for selling. In the space below, provide the noble purposes for your products/services.

1. _____

2. _____

3. _____

4. _____

5. _____

Tell a Story

Stories are merely our personal experiences shaped into a recounting or retelling of the event along with any insights, emotions or thoughts we have, or had, about the experience. Think about the last time you couldn't wait to tell a friend about something that happened at work, or on a first date, or at school, or a vacation. What did you feel when you were telling your friend about what happened? Did you raise your voice? Get excited? Did you wave your hands around or use body language to demonstrate some aspect of the event? Did you have a beginning, middle and end? Did you look for a reaction from your friend when you finished telling them what happened? If you did any of these things you were telling a story.

You want a sales story rather than a sales pitch because it's stories that stir people to action. Pitches shut them down. Stories are emotional connections to real events, real feelings, real fears and joys. They're not reports; they're not spreadsheets or bullet point slide presentations. They're actual events that reveal our vulnerability, our weaknesses, and our less than perfect abilities. They're a recounting of events that make us real.

Exercise #3

When we tell stories, we activate the right side, the creative and more receptive side of our customers' brains as well as our own. Stories also don't make customers feel like they're being threatened or "sold to."

Crafting a story isn't about learning a script. It's not about making something up either. When telling a story to a customer it needs to be real. You must be genuine when talking to your customer. You're not trying to trick, manipulate or use them. You're trying to connect with them. Crafting a story is about sharing a personal, meaningful and relevant story about something you've experienced that will help you connect with your customer.

There are four steps to building your sales story.

1. **Build a structure.** The beginning sets what is, and establishes credibility. The middle contrasts what is and what could be; and the end tells how amazing the future will be with your idea, solution or insight.
2. **Understand what will resonate with your audience or customer.** Nancy Duart, author, speaker and storyteller, mentions Steve Jobs' well-known iPhone launch speech and Dr. Martin Luther King Jr.'s "*I Have a Dream Speech*" because of the power of each of those speeches to connect with her audience.
3. **"Imagine and poetically describe an amazing future."** The whole point of telling a story is to get to the happy ending. That happy ending can be a solution, a lesson, an insight or a positive change of circumstances. Whatever the ending is, make it believable, achievable and memorable.
4. **Capture your customer's attention ASAP.** Perhaps the most famous beginning in movie history is the introduction to the movie 'Star Wars':

For this exercise, draft a short sales story that you could share with one of your prospects. Consider your average prospect and provide details of the story that you would tell the next prospect in order to build a meaningful and personal relationship with that person. Remember, your story does not need to long. Follow the steps above when crafting your story.

Now that you have your story, you're ready to break the ice. If you can do it successfully, humor is a good way to start. If humor isn't your thing, try honest compliments, or ask questions about a non-sales or non-product topic. Anything from the weather to a ring the customer is wearing, to a recent item in the news, sports, or upcoming holiday can be an icebreaker. The goal is to connect with the person and get them talking to you. Once you're talking and the ball is rolling you can shift or start a conversation about what problem or challenge they're trying to solve.

Putting Conversation Starters into Action

Starting a conversation takes practice. The more you start up conversations with anyone, the better your ice breaking skills are going to be. Remember the following steps when starting up a conversation.

1. **Determine what your noble purpose is.** A noble purpose doesn't have to be something that will win you humanitarian of the year or a Pulitzer.
2. **Think about some stories you could tell customers which they'd remember and which could spark interaction with them and, perhaps, a sale down the road.** If you don't already own and use whatever it is you're selling, perhaps now is the time to do that.
3. **Break the ice through humor and/or asking potential new customers questions about themselves.** This can be something as simple as sharing photos of your pet, or asking them if they've seen the latest movie, or if they're a sports fan.
4. **Ask them about their needs / wants.** Help him explore the pros and cons of each, including price.
5. **As you get to know them, look for a place to tell your story after you learn a bit about them.** When telling a story, don't 'one-up' your customer. It's about sharing common experiences.
6. **Listen for their story and then look for a way to contribute.** Listening for story means more than just listening to the words. It means listening for the intent behind the story.
7. **Guide the conversation by teaching your customer something, tailoring a solution, and then challenging them.** Studies show that customers gravitate towards salespeople who know their product's good points and bad, and who also know how to explain how to use the product and when to use it.

Exercise #4

After you have had a chance to put these techniques into practice, come back to this guidebook and note how the conversation starters went. Specifically note if you noticed any difference in your conversations versus your past conversations. Journaling your experiences will help you gain insight and also patterns of success and needed improvement areas.

_____

_____

_____

_____

_____

_____

_____

_____

_____

_____

_____

_____

_____

_____

_____

_____

_____

_____

CHAPTER 7

Awaken and Expand Your Network

Introduction

Today, the concept of networking has taken on a whole new meaning. It's so easy to sit behind our computers and make so-called connections with people we have never met. But these certainly aren't real connections. They are nothing but lazy, feeble attempts to build a network which does nothing to help our goals. Can you really be connected to someone you've never met and have no intention of meeting face to face? Absolutely not. Real networking requires effort and work. It requires taking steps to build relationships with the people you want to get to know.

So how can you go about building real, personal relationships? It helps to first understand what has changed in networking habits.

Today's Networking

Building out your network provides some immense opportunities. Networking is all about engagement with the people you meet. So what does engagement look like? If you're taking 100 percent of the responsibility for the relationship, then you should be a great listener. Building and using your network gives you a leg up in the sales process. The more people you know, the more people you have the potential to meet. And the more groups you interact with, the more opportunities you will have to meet people with whom you share common goals.

Exercise #1

For this exercise, answer the following questions regarding your current network.

1.	How many people are you currently connected with you through your online social networks (LinkedIn, Facebook, Google+, etc.)?
2.	How many of these people do or did you actually know in real life?
3.	How many of them do you make a constant effort to stay in touch with face-to-face?
4.	For the people in your networks who you don't know in real life, how many of them have you attempted to contact beyond accepting their connection request?
5.	Do you belong to any online thought leaderships groups? If so, do you participate in them?
6.	What kinds of people are included in your face-to-face network?

Face-to-Face Networking

Face-to-face networking today has virtually disappeared because of technology. Connecting with people face to face is becoming a lost art, but it doesn't have to be. With some effort on your part, you can create long-lasting relationships that matter to those with whom you connect.

Face-to-face meetings are essential in business relationships, particularly in the advent of face-to-face technology like Skype. Researchers discovered that there are three reasons situations in which face-to-face meetings are the best approach: "to capture attention;" "to inspire a positive emotional climate;" and "to build human networks and relationships."

So how can we make the most of face-to-face meetings? It essentially boils down to making sure that you're listening effectively to the client and that distractions for the client are minimized as much as you can do so. This will enable the client to listen to you more closely as well.

Exercise #2

One important aspect of face-to-face networking is being involved in and joining different groups. This could be your local Chamber of Commerce, Church groups, industry-related groups and more.

For this exercise, research at least five groups that you could join. Remember, the more people you meet, the greater your network will be and the more sales you are likely to make. For each group, provide a brief description of the group.

	NETWORKING GROUP	CHARACTERISTICS
1.		
2.		
3.		
4.		
5.		

Online Networking

Because of the Internet, we can connect with potential clients all over the world. This creates immeasurable opportunities to share and connect. Those who don't use their online networks are missing out in so many ways.

So how can you make the most of your online network? It all starts with what you share. Of course, what's meaningful to one person may not mean anything to the next, so it's helpful to learn different techniques for meeting, sharing with, and interacting with people in your online networks. As a guideline, we'll look at some ideas for connecting with both people you know and don't know.

For Someone You Know

In some cases, you may have connected with someone you have met a time or two through LinkedIn or one of the other social networks. In other cases, you may have allowed a relationship to slump by ignoring it or being complacent about it. Whatever the reason you feel like you want to develop a relationship with someone you know, there are some simple ways to go about it.

It's good to have a general script in mind when you do this. Here are the basic elements of a proper script:

1. A personalized welcome.
2. A suggestion to connect for a mutually beneficial relationship.
3. And a thank you for reading your message / accepting your connection request, or whatever else makes sense here.

Exercise #3

For this exercise, create a brief script that you would send to someone you know in an online networking site. Write your script below:

_____

_____

_____

_____

_____

_____

_____

_____

_____

_____

_____

For Someone You DON'T KNOW

If you're trying to get to know someone you've never met before, then the script will obviously go quite a bit differently. You'll need more of an introduction because neither you nor the other person knows anything about each other. You don't have some commonality upon which to build because this is someone you haven't met before. However, if you're the one making the first move, then you've probably read the other person's online profile. If so, then there's a reason you felt compelled to reach out to the other person. You may have noticed some sort of commonality upon which to build, but you've then got to introduce that commonality to the other person before you can move forward. Here are the basic building blocks of a script to introduce yourself to someone you have never met:

1. A personalized introduction.
2. In the body of the message, identify something in the person's profile that you either find interesting or have in common.
3. Suggest connecting for a mutually beneficial relationship.
4. Thank them for taking the time to read your invitation.
5. Suggest a "next step" to connect further.

Exercise #4

For this exercise, create a brief script that you would send to someone you do not know in an online networking site. Write your script below:

_____

_____

_____

_____

_____

_____

_____

_____

_____

_____

_____

_____

_____

_____

_____

_____

Grow Your Online Through Groups

So where might you meet people who would be good additions to your network? Perhaps the simplest way is to approach them through LinkedIn by using a mutual connection. However, the mutual connection must be someone you already have a good face-to-face relationship with. If you don't have a relationship with your mutual connection and don't feel like that connection is a good person to add into your real network (not your virtual one), then it may be best to not even acknowledge that you both know the same person. The topic could come up in conversation at some point if you ask how the person you're connecting with how they know the person you both know. But if it does, it should be later in the relationship, possibly as a talking point a few conversations in.

Aside from simply running across their profile on LinkedIn, you could also join some groups. No matter where you are in your career, you can benefit greatly from joining groups, both in the real world and on LinkedIn. Even people who are very successful in their careers fine a benefit in joining groups.

When it comes to online groups, there is nearly an endless supply. So how do you go about choosing which groups to become a member of? Here are some things to look for. You might consider industry-specific groups like healthcare, retail, or something else. The group should be a place where you can meet potential customers or where you have something in common with the people who belong to the group.

There are also local and regional groups, which can be of great benefit because you have more opportunities for getting to know the members on a face-to-face basis. And then there are solution-specific groups.

Exercise #5

For this exercise, if you do not have a LinkedIn account, you will need to create one. After creating your LinkedIn account, search for groups given the guidelines above. In the area provided below, list the groups you have joined and what you feel is the potential benefit (in terms of networking) of these groups. You should try to join at least five groups.

	GROUP	BENEFITS OF JOINING GROUP
1.		
2.		
3.		
4.		
5.		

When networking, remember these important thoughts.

1. **Don't shirk face-to-face time.** The best way to keep in contact with the people you meet is to give them a call from time to time and ask to meet face to face.
2. **Always be genuine when interacting with others.** People sense when you're being fake, so don't even try to be real if you don't feel it.
3. **Find ways to make yourself memorable to those you meet.** This is especially true at big networking events where you meet hundreds of new people.
4. **Show gratitude.** Always thank the people you reach out to as potential additions to your network.
5. **Suggest connecting for a mutually beneficial relationship.** Most people have online networks that they never use and don't have any intention to use.
6. **When trying to connect with someone you don't know, introduce yourself.** It takes a bit more of an introduction to connect with others you don't know, but it can be done.
7. **Target a few different types of groups you would like to join.** Groups are an excellent way to expand your network.
8. **Use online groups to grow your influence.** After you join some online groups, engage with the other group members by answering questions, asking questions, and just taking part in the conversations.
9. **Be the first to engage with the individuals you want to meet.** In most cases on online networks, people are pretty complacent in terms of their face-to-face relationships with the people in their networks. Be the first to reach out if you want to have a real, mutually beneficial relationship with someone in your network or someone who belongs to the same group as you.

CHAPTER 8

Action Steps to Take Conversations to the Next Level

Introduction

By now you must be asking yourself: is this a book about sales or about relationships? The answer is both! You can't have a million dollar sales conversation without a relationship. In fact, once you become skilled at developing relationships, million dollar sales conversations just sort of happen—almost without any noticeable effort on your part.

But in reality, you do put effort in when you do things honestly. You pour your heart and soul into a relationship in a way that was so natural you didn't even feel in the beginning that you were aiming for a million dollar sales conversation. The most lucrative conversations are those that happen naturally as a result of a good relationship built on a solid foundation of trust and exchange.

The Domino Effect

Each step builds upon the next. As one domino touches the next, it touches the next one, and so on—all the way through the chain.

And a relationship is the first domino.

Step 1: A is for Attitude

In order to have good relationships, you must have a good attitude.

Step 2: Set Goals and Stick to Them

If you have a good attitude, it will be easy for you to write down your goals and achieve them.

Step 3: Listen Actively

In order to help your customer meet his goals, you must be a great listener so that you can provide the best possible solution.

Step 4: Be an Encourager

The more you listen carefully, the more you will realize that sometimes encouragement is appropriate. Remember: great things come from great relationships!

Step 5: Make Successful Small Talk for Continued Success

Encouragement leads to further exchange and a deepening relationship, and the further you take your relationship, the more you'll find the need to be able to make small talk.

Step 6: Stretch Your Network

Checking in with your contacts and making small talk from time to time is the best way to stay in touch and grow your network, expand it, and put it to work. The more you grow your relationships, the more new people you will find that you meet. Your contacts will want to introduce you to people they think you can help. They'll also want you to meet people they think can help you.

Get to Work

All of this may seem like a lot to remember, but if you take the time to work on these things, soon they will become second-nature to you. So just pick one thing you feel needs the most work right now and focus on that, keeping the other things tucked away in the back of your mind.

Your own million dollar sales conversation is just around the corner. Start just one new relationship today and see where it takes you!

In the pages that follow, take time to come back to the guidebook and journal about the conversations that you have. The more time that we take assessing our conversations, the better conversations we will, the stronger our relationships will be, and the more million-dollar sales conversations we will start!

JOURNAL NOTES

JOURNAL NOTES

JOURNAL NOTES

JOURNAL NOTES

JOURNAL NOTES

JOURNAL NOTES

JOURNAL NOTES

JOURNAL NOTES

JOURNAL NOTES

JOURNAL NOTES

JOURNAL NOTES

JOURNAL NOTES

www.ingramcontent.com/pod-product-compliance
Lightning Source LLC
Chambersburg PA
CBHW051420200326
41520CB00023B/7313